50 Fish and Seafood Recipes

By: Kelly Johnson

Table of Contents

- Grilled Salmon with Lemon Butter
- Shrimp Scampi
- Baked Cod with Garlic and Herbs
- Spicy Tuna Tartare
- Clam Chowder
- Fish Tacos with Mango Salsa
- Garlic Butter Shrimp Pasta
- Blackened Catfish
- Crab Cakes with Remoulade Sauce
- Fish and Chips
- Thai Red Curry Shrimp
- Lemon Garlic Butter Lobster
- Shrimp Fried Rice
- Pan-Seared Scallops
- Miso Glazed Black Cod
- Seafood Paella
- Grilled Swordfish Steaks
- Lemon Dill Baked Trout
- Spaghetti Vongole (Clam Spaghetti)
- Mediterranean Shrimp Skewers
- Seafood Gumbo
- Baked Halibut with Tomato Salsa
- Ceviche with Lime and Cilantro
- Shrimp and Grits
- Fish Piccata
- Smoked Salmon Bagels
- Lobster Roll
- Crab Linguine
- Sesame-Crusted Ahi Tuna
- Fish Curry with Coconut Milk
- Garlic Roasted Shrimp
- Grilled Octopus with Lemon
- Baked Mahi-Mahi with Pineapple Salsa
- Fish Chowder
- Thai Coconut Shrimp Soup
- Salmon Quiche

- Prawn Korma
- Lemon Herb Grilled Sardines
- Shrimp Ceviche Tostadas
- Grilled Tuna Steaks with Soy Marinade
- Fish En Papillote (Fish in Parchment)
- Baked Salmon with Honey Mustard Glaze
- Szechuan Spicy Shrimp
- Fish Burger with Avocado
- Crab and Corn Chowder
- Teriyaki Salmon
- Zesty Shrimp Tacos
- Seared Bass with Citrus Sauce
- Grilled Shrimp Caesar Salad
- Stuffed Squid with Rice and Herbs

Grilled Salmon with Lemon Butter

Ingredients:

- 4 salmon fillets (6 oz each)
- 2 tablespoons olive oil
- Salt and pepper, to taste
- 2 tablespoons fresh lemon juice
- 2 tablespoons unsalted butter
- 2 cloves garlic, minced
- 1 tablespoon fresh parsley, chopped (optional for garnish)
- Lemon wedges, for serving

Instructions:

1. **Prepare the Marinade:**
   - In a small bowl, whisk together the olive oil, lemon juice, salt, and pepper.
2. **Marinate the Salmon:**
   - Place the salmon fillets in a shallow dish and pour the marinade over them. Let the salmon marinate for about 15-30 minutes.
3. **Preheat the Grill:**
   - Preheat your grill to medium-high heat (about 400°F to 450°F).
4. **Grill the Salmon:**
   - Remove the salmon from the marinade and let any excess liquid drip off.
   - Place the fillets skin-side down on the grill. Grill for about 4-6 minutes per side, or until the salmon flakes easily with a fork and reaches an internal temperature of 145°F.
5. **Make the Lemon Butter:**
   - While the salmon is grilling, melt the butter in a small saucepan over medium heat.
   - Add the minced garlic and sauté for about 1 minute, until fragrant.
   - Remove from heat and stir in the lemon juice.
6. **Serve:**
   - Once the salmon is done, transfer the fillets to a serving platter. Drizzle the garlic lemon butter over the top.
   - Garnish with chopped parsley, if desired, and serve with lemon wedges.

Shrimp Scampi

Ingredients:

- 1 pound large shrimp, peeled and deveined
- 4 tablespoons unsalted butter
- 2 tablespoons olive oil
- 4 cloves garlic, minced
- 1/4 teaspoon red pepper flakes (adjust to taste)
- 1/2 cup dry white wine
- 1 tablespoon fresh lemon juice
- Salt and pepper, to taste
- 1/4 cup fresh parsley, chopped
- Cooked pasta, for serving (optional)

Instructions:

1. **Sauté the Garlic:**
    - In a large skillet over medium heat, melt the butter and olive oil together.
    - Add the minced garlic and red pepper flakes, sautéing for about 1 minute until fragrant.
2. **Cook the Shrimp:**
    - Add the shrimp to the skillet and season with salt and pepper. Cook for about 2-3 minutes until the shrimp turn pink and opaque.
3. **Add Wine and Lemon Juice:**
    - Pour in the white wine and lemon juice, stirring to combine. Let it simmer for 2-3 minutes until slightly reduced.
4. **Garnish and Serve:**
    - Stir in the chopped parsley and adjust seasoning if needed.
    - Serve over cooked pasta, if desired, with extra lemon wedges.

Baked Cod with Garlic and Herbs

Ingredients:

- 4 cod fillets (6 oz each)
- 4 tablespoons olive oil
- 4 cloves garlic, minced
- 1 teaspoon dried oregano
- 1 teaspoon dried thyme
- Salt and pepper, to taste
- Juice of 1 lemon
- Fresh parsley, for garnish

Instructions:

1. **Preheat the Oven:**
   - Preheat your oven to 400°F (200°C).
2. **Prepare the Herb Mixture:**
   - In a small bowl, combine the olive oil, minced garlic, oregano, thyme, salt, and pepper.
3. **Coat the Cod:**
   - Place the cod fillets in a baking dish and pour the herb mixture over them. Squeeze lemon juice on top.
4. **Bake:**
   - Bake for 15-20 minutes, or until the fish flakes easily with a fork and is opaque.
5. **Garnish and Serve:**
   - Garnish with fresh parsley and serve with lemon wedges.

Spicy Tuna Tartare

Ingredients:

- 1 pound sushi-grade tuna, diced
- 2 tablespoons soy sauce
- 1 tablespoon sesame oil
- 1 tablespoon Sriracha (adjust to taste)
- 1 teaspoon grated fresh ginger
- 1 avocado, diced
- 1 green onion, sliced
- 1 tablespoon sesame seeds
- Wonton chips or tortilla chips, for serving

Instructions:

1. **Prepare the Tuna:**
   - In a medium bowl, combine the diced tuna, soy sauce, sesame oil, Sriracha, and grated ginger. Mix gently to coat the tuna.
2. **Add Avocado and Green Onion:**
   - Gently fold in the diced avocado and sliced green onion.
3. **Serve:**
   - Transfer the tuna tartare to a serving dish, sprinkle with sesame seeds, and serve with wonton chips or tortilla chips.

Clam Chowder

Ingredients:

- 4 slices bacon, chopped
- 1 onion, diced
- 2 cloves garlic, minced
- 2 medium potatoes, diced
- 1 cup heavy cream
- 1 cup milk
- 2 cans (6.5 oz each) chopped clams, drained (reserve liquid)
- 1 teaspoon dried thyme
- Salt and pepper, to taste
- Fresh parsley, for garnish

Instructions:

1. **Cook the Bacon:**
   - In a large pot, cook the bacon over medium heat until crispy. Remove and set aside, leaving the drippings.
2. **Sauté the Vegetables:**
   - Add the onion and garlic to the pot, cooking until softened. Add the potatoes and reserved clam liquid, bringing to a boil.
3. **Simmer:**
   - Reduce heat and simmer until potatoes are tender, about 15 minutes.
4. **Add Cream and Clams:**
   - Stir in the heavy cream, milk, clams, thyme, salt, and pepper. Heat through without boiling.
5. **Serve:**
   - Garnish with bacon and parsley before serving.

Fish Tacos with Mango Salsa

Ingredients:

- 1 pound white fish fillets (like tilapia or cod)
- 2 tablespoons olive oil
- 1 teaspoon chili powder
- Salt and pepper, to taste
- 8 small corn tortillas
- 1 cup shredded cabbage

Mango Salsa:

- 1 ripe mango, diced
- 1/2 red onion, diced
- 1 jalapeño, minced
- Juice of 1 lime
- Salt, to taste

Instructions:

1. **Prepare the Salsa:**
   - Combine mango, onion, jalapeño, lime juice, and salt in a bowl. Set aside.
2. **Cook the Fish:**
   - Season fish with olive oil, chili powder, salt, and pepper. Cook in a skillet over medium heat for about 4-5 minutes per side, until cooked through.
3. **Assemble Tacos:**
   - Warm tortillas, then top with fish, shredded cabbage, and mango salsa.

Garlic Butter Shrimp Pasta

Ingredients:

- 8 ounces linguine or spaghetti
- 1 pound shrimp, peeled and deveined
- 4 tablespoons unsalted butter
- 4 cloves garlic, minced
- 1/2 teaspoon red pepper flakes (optional)
- 1/4 cup parsley, chopped
- Salt and pepper, to taste
- Juice of 1 lemon

Instructions:

1. **Cook Pasta:**
   - Cook pasta according to package instructions; drain and set aside.
2. **Sauté Shrimp:**
   - In a large skillet, melt butter over medium heat. Add garlic and red pepper flakes, cooking until fragrant.
3. **Add Shrimp:**
   - Add shrimp, cooking until pink and opaque, about 2-3 minutes per side.
4. **Combine:**
   - Add cooked pasta, parsley, salt, pepper, and lemon juice. Toss to combine.

Blackened Catfish

Ingredients:

- 4 catfish fillets
- 2 tablespoons paprika
- 1 tablespoon cayenne pepper
- 1 tablespoon garlic powder
- 1 tablespoon onion powder
- 1 teaspoon dried thyme
- 1 teaspoon salt
- 1/2 teaspoon black pepper
- 4 tablespoons butter, melted

Instructions:

1. **Prepare the Spice Mixture:**
   - Mix paprika, cayenne, garlic powder, onion powder, thyme, salt, and pepper in a bowl.
2. **Coat the Fish:**
   - Brush catfish fillets with melted butter and coat with the spice mixture.
3. **Cook:**
   - In a hot skillet, cook the catfish for about 4-5 minutes per side until blackened and cooked through.

Crab Cakes with Remoulade Sauce

Ingredients:

- 1 pound lump crab meat
- 1/2 cup breadcrumbs
- 1/4 cup mayonnaise
- 1 egg
- 2 tablespoons Dijon mustard
- 1 tablespoon Worcestershire sauce
- 1 tablespoon fresh parsley, chopped
- Salt and pepper, to taste
- Oil for frying

Remoulade Sauce:

- 1/2 cup mayonnaise
- 1 tablespoon Dijon mustard
- 1 tablespoon lemon juice
- 1 tablespoon capers, chopped
- 1 teaspoon hot sauce

Instructions:

1. **Prepare the Remoulade:**
    - Combine all remoulade ingredients in a bowl; set aside.
2. **Make the Crab Cakes:**
    - In a large bowl, combine crab meat, breadcrumbs, mayonnaise, egg, mustard, Worcestershire sauce, parsley, salt, and pepper. Form into patties.
3. **Cook:**
    - Heat oil in a skillet over medium heat. Fry crab cakes for 4-5 minutes per side until golden brown. Serve with remoulade sauce.

Fish and Chips

Ingredients:

- 4 white fish fillets (like cod or haddock)
- 1 cup all-purpose flour
- 1 cup beer
- 1 teaspoon baking powder
- Salt and pepper, to taste
- Oil for frying
- 4 large potatoes, cut into fries

Instructions:

1. **Prepare the Fries:**
    - Preheat oil in a deep fryer or large pot. Fry potatoes until golden and crispy; remove and drain.
2. **Make the Batter:**
    - In a bowl, mix flour, beer, baking powder, salt, and pepper until smooth.
3. **Coat and Fry Fish:**
    - Dip fish fillets in the batter and fry until golden brown, about 4-5 minutes. Drain on paper towels.
4. **Serve:**
    - Serve fish with fries and tartar sauce if desired.

Thai Red Curry Shrimp

Ingredients:

- 1 pound shrimp, peeled and deveined
- 2 tablespoons red curry paste
- 1 can (13.5 oz) coconut milk
- 1 cup bell peppers, sliced
- 1 cup snap peas
- 2 tablespoons fish sauce
- Fresh basil, for garnish
- Cooked jasmine rice, for serving

Instructions:

1. **Cook the Curry Paste:**
   - In a large skillet, cook red curry paste over medium heat for 1-2 minutes until fragrant.
2. **Add Coconut Milk:**
   - Stir in coconut milk, bell peppers, and snap peas. Simmer for about 5 minutes.
3. **Add Shrimp:**
   - Add shrimp and fish sauce, cooking until shrimp is pink and cooked through, about 3-4 minutes.
4. **Serve:**
   - Garnish with fresh basil and serve over jasmine rice.

Lemon Garlic Butter Lobster

Ingredients:

- 2 lobsters (about 1.5 pounds each), split in half
- 6 tablespoons unsalted butter
- 4 cloves garlic, minced
- Juice of 1 lemon
- Salt and pepper, to taste
- Fresh parsley, for garnish

Instructions:

1. **Preheat Oven:**
   - Preheat your oven to 425°F (220°C).
2. **Prepare the Lobster:**
   - Place lobster halves on a baking sheet, meat side up.
3. **Make the Garlic Butter:**
   - In a small saucepan, melt butter over low heat. Add garlic, lemon juice, salt, and pepper.
4. **Brush Lobster:**
   - Brush lobster meat with garlic butter, then bake for 12-15 minutes until cooked through.
5. **Serve:**
   - Garnish with fresh parsley before serving.

Shrimp Fried Rice

Ingredients:

- 2 cups cooked rice (preferably day-old)
- 1 pound shrimp, peeled and deveined
- 2 tablespoons vegetable oil
- 3 green onions, chopped
- 2 cloves garlic, minced
- 2 eggs, beaten
- 3 tablespoons soy sauce
- 1 tablespoon sesame oil
- Salt and pepper, to taste
- Peas and carrots (optional)

Instructions:

1. **Heat Oil:**
    - In a large skillet or wok, heat vegetable oil over medium-high heat.
2. **Cook Shrimp:**
    - Add shrimp and cook until pink and opaque, about 2-3 minutes. Remove and set aside.
3. **Sauté Vegetables:**
    - In the same skillet, add garlic and green onions, cooking until fragrant. If using, add peas and carrots.
4. **Add Eggs:**
    - Push vegetables to the side, add beaten eggs, and scramble until cooked.
5. **Combine:**
    - Add cooked rice, shrimp, soy sauce, sesame oil, salt, and pepper. Stir-fry for 3-4 minutes until heated through.

Pan-Seared Scallops

Ingredients:

- 1 pound sea scallops
- Salt and pepper, to taste
- 2 tablespoons olive oil
- 2 tablespoons butter
- 2 cloves garlic, minced
- Lemon wedges, for serving

Instructions:

1. **Prepare Scallops:**
   - Pat scallops dry with paper towels and season with salt and pepper.
2. **Heat Oil:**
   - In a skillet, heat olive oil over medium-high heat until shimmering.
3. **Sear Scallops:**
   - Add scallops to the skillet, cooking for about 2-3 minutes on each side until golden brown. Remove and set aside.
4. **Make Sauce:**
   - In the same skillet, add butter and garlic, cooking until fragrant. Drizzle over scallops and serve with lemon wedges.

Miso Glazed Black Cod

Ingredients:

- 4 black cod fillets
- 1/4 cup miso paste
- 1/4 cup sake
- 1/4 cup mirin
- 2 tablespoons sugar
- Sesame seeds, for garnish
- Green onions, for garnish

Instructions:

1. **Make Marinade:**
    - In a bowl, whisk together miso paste, sake, mirin, and sugar until smooth.
2. **Marinate Cod:**
    - Coat black cod fillets in the marinade, cover, and refrigerate for at least 4 hours or overnight.
3. **Preheat Oven:**
    - Preheat your oven to 400°F (200°C).
4. **Bake:**
    - Place marinated fillets on a baking sheet lined with parchment paper. Bake for 10-12 minutes until cooked through.
5. **Garnish:**
    - Sprinkle with sesame seeds and green onions before serving.

Seafood Paella

Ingredients:

- 2 tablespoons olive oil
- 1 onion, diced
- 2 cloves garlic, minced
- 1 bell pepper, diced
- 1 cup Arborio rice
- 1 teaspoon smoked paprika
- 1/2 teaspoon saffron threads
- 4 cups seafood stock
- 1 pound shrimp, peeled and deveined
- 1 pound mussels, cleaned
- 1 cup peas
- Lemon wedges, for serving

Instructions:

1. **Sauté Vegetables:**
    - In a large paella pan or skillet, heat olive oil over medium heat. Add onion, garlic, and bell pepper, cooking until softened.
2. **Add Rice and Spices:**
    - Stir in Arborio rice, paprika, and saffron, cooking for 1-2 minutes.
3. **Add Stock:**
    - Pour in seafood stock, bringing to a boil. Reduce heat to low and simmer for 10 minutes.
4. **Add Seafood:**
    - Add shrimp, mussels, and peas, cooking until shrimp are pink and mussels open, about 5-7 minutes.
5. **Serve:**
    - Serve with lemon wedges.

Grilled Swordfish Steaks

Ingredients:

- 4 swordfish steaks
- 1/4 cup olive oil
- 2 tablespoons lemon juice
- 2 cloves garlic, minced
- Salt and pepper, to taste
- Fresh parsley, for garnish

Instructions:

1. **Prepare Marinade:**
   - In a bowl, whisk together olive oil, lemon juice, garlic, salt, and pepper.
2. **Marinate Fish:**
   - Place swordfish steaks in a shallow dish and pour marinade over. Refrigerate for 30 minutes.
3. **Preheat Grill:**
   - Preheat the grill to medium-high heat.
4. **Grill:**
   - Grill swordfish for about 5-6 minutes per side until cooked through.
5. **Serve:**
   - Garnish with fresh parsley before serving.

Lemon Dill Baked Trout

Ingredients:

- 4 trout fillets
- 2 tablespoons olive oil
- Juice of 1 lemon
- 2 tablespoons fresh dill, chopped
- Salt and pepper, to taste
- Lemon slices, for garnish

Instructions:

1. **Preheat Oven:**
    - Preheat your oven to 375°F (190°C).
2. **Prepare Trout:**
    - Place trout fillets on a baking sheet. Drizzle with olive oil and lemon juice. Season with dill, salt, and pepper.
3. **Bake:**
    - Bake for 15-20 minutes until fish flakes easily with a fork.
4. **Serve:**
    - Garnish with lemon slices.

Spaghetti Vongole (Clam Spaghetti)

Ingredients:

- 8 ounces spaghetti
- 2 tablespoons olive oil
- 4 cloves garlic, minced
- 1/2 teaspoon red pepper flakes
- 1 cup white wine
- 2 cans (10 oz each) baby clams, drained (reserve liquid)
- 1/4 cup parsley, chopped
- Salt and pepper, to taste
- Lemon wedges, for serving

Instructions:

1. **Cook Pasta:**
   - Cook spaghetti according to package instructions; drain and reserve some pasta water.
2. **Sauté Garlic:**
   - In a large skillet, heat olive oil over medium heat. Add garlic and red pepper flakes, cooking until fragrant.
3. **Add Wine and Clams:**
   - Pour in white wine and clam liquid, simmering for about 5 minutes. Add clams and cook until heated through.
4. **Combine:**
   - Add cooked spaghetti to the skillet, tossing to combine. If needed, add reserved pasta water for desired consistency.
5. **Serve:**
   - Garnish with parsley and serve with lemon wedges.

Mediterranean Shrimp Skewers

Ingredients:

- 1 pound shrimp, peeled and deveined
- 1/4 cup olive oil
- Juice of 1 lemon
- 2 cloves garlic, minced
- 1 teaspoon oregano
- Salt and pepper, to taste
- Wooden skewers, soaked in water

Instructions:

1. **Prepare Marinade:**
   - In a bowl, whisk together olive oil, lemon juice, garlic, oregano, salt, and pepper.
2. **Marinate Shrimp:**
   - Add shrimp to the marinade and let sit for 30 minutes.
3. **Preheat Grill:**
   - Preheat grill to medium-high heat.
4. **Skewer and Grill:**
   - Thread shrimp onto skewers. Grill for about 2-3 minutes per side until shrimp are cooked through.
5. **Serve:**
   - Serve warm with your favorite dipping sauce.

Seafood Gumbo

Ingredients:

- 1/2 cup vegetable oil
- 1/2 cup flour
- 1 onion, diced
- 1 bell pepper, diced
- 2 celery stalks, diced
- 4 cloves garlic, minced
- 1 pound andouille sausage, sliced
- 1 pound shrimp, peeled and deveined
- 1 pound crab meat
- 4 cups chicken stock
- 1 can (14.5 oz) diced tomatoes
- 2 teaspoons Cajun seasoning
- 2 bay leaves
- Salt and pepper, to taste
- Cooked rice, for serving
- Green onions, for garnish

Instructions:

1. **Make Roux:**
   - In a large pot, heat oil over medium heat. Stir in flour, cooking until it turns dark brown, about 20-25 minutes.
2. **Add Vegetables:**
   - Stir in onion, bell pepper, celery, and garlic, cooking until softened.
3. **Combine Ingredients:**
   - Add sausage, shrimp, crab meat, chicken stock, diced tomatoes, Cajun seasoning, bay leaves, salt, and pepper.
4. **Simmer:**
   - Bring to a boil, then reduce heat and simmer for 30-40 minutes.
5. **Serve:**
   - Serve over cooked rice and garnish with green onions.

Baked Halibut with Tomato Salsa

Ingredients:

- 4 halibut fillets
- Salt and pepper, to taste
- 2 tablespoons olive oil
- 1 cup cherry tomatoes, halved
- 1/4 cup red onion, diced
- 2 tablespoons fresh cilantro, chopped
- Juice of 1 lime

Instructions:

1. **Preheat Oven:**
   - Preheat oven to 400°F (200°C).
2. **Prepare Salsa:**
   - In a bowl, mix cherry tomatoes, red onion, cilantro, lime juice, salt, and pepper. Set aside.
3. **Bake Halibut:**
   - Place halibut fillets in a baking dish, drizzle with olive oil, and season with salt and pepper. Bake for 15-20 minutes until cooked through.
4. **Serve:**
   - Top halibut with tomato salsa before serving.

Ceviche with Lime and Cilantro

Ingredients:

- 1 pound fresh white fish (such as tilapia), diced
- Juice of 4 limes
- 1/2 red onion, thinly sliced
- 1 tomato, diced
- 1 jalapeño, minced
- 1/4 cup fresh cilantro, chopped
- Salt and pepper, to taste

Instructions:

1. **Marinate Fish:**
    - In a bowl, combine diced fish and lime juice. Cover and refrigerate for 2-3 hours until fish is opaque.
2. **Add Vegetables:**
    - Stir in red onion, tomato, jalapeño, cilantro, salt, and pepper.
3. **Serve:**
    - Serve chilled with tortilla chips.

Shrimp and Grits

Ingredients:

- 1 cup grits
- 4 cups water
- 1 pound shrimp, peeled and deveined
- 4 slices bacon, chopped
- 1/2 cup heavy cream
- 2 cloves garlic, minced
- 1 teaspoon Cajun seasoning
- Salt and pepper, to taste
- Green onions, for garnish

Instructions:

1. **Cook Grits:**
   - In a pot, bring water to a boil. Stir in grits, reduce heat, and simmer until thickened, about 20 minutes.
2. **Cook Bacon:**
   - In a skillet, cook bacon until crispy. Remove bacon and set aside.
3. **Cook Shrimp:**
   - In the same skillet, add shrimp, garlic, Cajun seasoning, salt, and pepper. Cook until shrimp are pink.
4. **Combine:**
   - Stir heavy cream into the shrimp mixture and combine with cooked grits.
5. **Serve:**
   - Serve shrimp over grits, garnished with bacon and green onions.

Fish Piccata

Ingredients:

- 4 fish fillets (such as sole or tilapia)
- Salt and pepper, to taste
- 1/2 cup flour
- 2 tablespoons olive oil
- 2 tablespoons butter
- 1/2 cup white wine
- Juice of 1 lemon
- 1/4 cup capers
- Fresh parsley, for garnish

Instructions:

1. **Prepare Fish:**
   - Season fish fillets with salt and pepper, then dredge in flour.
2. **Cook Fish:**
   - In a skillet, heat olive oil and butter over medium heat. Add fish and cook until golden, about 3-4 minutes per side. Remove and set aside.
3. **Make Sauce:**
   - In the same skillet, add white wine, lemon juice, and capers, simmering for 2-3 minutes.
4. **Combine:**
   - Return fish to the skillet, spooning sauce over the top.
5. **Serve:**
   - Garnish with fresh parsley before serving.

Smoked Salmon Bagels

Ingredients:

- 4 bagels, sliced
- 8 ounces cream cheese
- 8 ounces smoked salmon
- 1/4 red onion, thinly sliced
- 1/4 cup capers
- Fresh dill, for garnish
- Lemon wedges, for serving

Instructions:

1. **Prepare Bagels:**
   - Toast bagels until golden brown.
2. **Spread Cream Cheese:**
   - Spread cream cheese evenly on each bagel half.
3. **Layer Ingredients:**
   - Top with smoked salmon, red onion, and capers.
4. **Serve:**
   - Garnish with dill and serve with lemon wedges.

Lobster Roll

Ingredients:

- 2 lobster tails, cooked and chopped
- 1/4 cup mayonnaise
- 1 tablespoon lemon juice
- 1 tablespoon fresh parsley, chopped
- Salt and pepper, to taste
- 4 hot dog buns
- Butter, for toasting buns

Instructions:

1. **Prepare Filling:**
    - In a bowl, combine lobster, mayonnaise, lemon juice, parsley, salt, and pepper.
2. **Toast Buns:**
    - Butter hot dog buns and toast on a skillet until golden.
3. **Assemble:**
    - Fill each bun with lobster mixture.
4. **Serve:**
    - Serve immediately.

Crab Linguine

Ingredients:

- 8 ounces linguine
- 2 tablespoons olive oil
- 2 cloves garlic, minced
- 1 pound lump crab meat
- 1/2 cup heavy cream
- Juice of 1 lemon
- 1/4 cup fresh parsley, chopped
- Salt and pepper, to taste

Instructions:

1. **Cook Pasta:**
   - Cook linguine according to package instructions; drain.
2. **Sauté Garlic:**
   - In a skillet, heat olive oil over medium heat. Add garlic and cook until fragrant.
3. **Add Crab:**
   - Stir in crab meat, heavy cream, lemon juice, salt, and pepper. Cook until heated through.
4. **Combine:**
   - Toss cooked linguine with crab mixture.
5. **Serve:**
   - Garnish with parsley before serving.

Sesame-Crusted Ahi Tuna

Ingredients:

- 2 ahi tuna steaks
- 1/4 cup sesame seeds
- Salt and pepper, to taste
- 2 tablespoons soy sauce
- 1 tablespoon olive oil
- Wasabi and soy sauce, for serving

Instructions:

1. **Prepare Tuna:**
   - Season tuna steaks with salt and pepper. Dip each side in soy sauce, then coat with sesame seeds.
2. **Heat Oil:**
   - In a skillet, heat olive oil over medium-high heat.
3. **Sear Tuna:**
   - Sear tuna for about 1-2 minutes on each side, leaving the center rare.
4. **Serve:**
   - Slice and serve with wasabi and soy sauce.

Fish Curry with Coconut Milk

Ingredients:

- 1 pound white fish fillets, cut into chunks
- 1 can (14 oz) coconut milk
- 2 tablespoons curry paste
- 1 onion, chopped
- 2 cloves garlic, minced
- 1 tablespoon ginger, minced
- 1 bell pepper, sliced
- 1 tablespoon fish sauce
- Juice of 1 lime
- Fresh cilantro, for garnish

Instructions:

1. **Sauté Vegetables:**
    - In a large pan, sauté onion, garlic, and ginger until fragrant.
2. **Add Curry Paste:**
    - Stir in curry paste and cook for 1 minute.
3. **Combine Ingredients:**
    - Add coconut milk, fish sauce, and bell pepper. Simmer for 5 minutes.
4. **Cook Fish:**
    - Add fish chunks and simmer until cooked through, about 5-7 minutes.
5. **Serve:**
    - Drizzle with lime juice and garnish with cilantro.

Garlic Roasted Shrimp

Ingredients:

- 1 pound shrimp, peeled and deveined
- 4 cloves garlic, minced
- 1/4 cup olive oil
- Salt and pepper, to taste
- 1 teaspoon paprika
- Fresh parsley, for garnish

Instructions:

1. **Preheat Oven:**
   - Preheat oven to 400°F (200°C).
2. **Prepare Shrimp:**
   - In a bowl, combine shrimp, garlic, olive oil, salt, pepper, and paprika.
3. **Roast Shrimp:**
   - Spread shrimp on a baking sheet and roast for 8-10 minutes until pink.
4. **Serve:**
   - Garnish with fresh parsley before serving.

Grilled Octopus with Lemon

Ingredients:

- 1 pound octopus, cleaned
- 1/4 cup olive oil
- Juice of 2 lemons
- 3 cloves garlic, minced
- Salt and pepper, to taste
- Fresh parsley, for garnish

Instructions:

1. **Prepare Marinade:**
    - In a bowl, mix olive oil, lemon juice, garlic, salt, and pepper.
2. **Marinate Octopus:**
    - Place octopus in marinade for at least 1 hour.
3. **Grill Octopus:**
    - Preheat grill to medium-high heat. Grill octopus for 3-4 minutes on each side.
4. **Serve:**
    - Garnish with fresh parsley and lemon wedges.

Baked Mahi-Mahi with Pineapple Salsa

Ingredients:

- 4 mahi-mahi fillets
- Salt and pepper, to taste
- 1 tablespoon olive oil
- 1 cup pineapple, diced
- 1/2 red onion, diced
- 1/4 cup cilantro, chopped
- Juice of 1 lime

Instructions:

1. **Preheat Oven:**
   - Preheat oven to 375°F (190°C).
2. **Prepare Salsa:**
   - In a bowl, combine pineapple, red onion, cilantro, lime juice, salt, and pepper.
3. **Bake Fish:**
   - Place mahi-mahi fillets in a baking dish, drizzle with olive oil, and season. Bake for 15-20 minutes until cooked through.
4. **Serve:**
   - Top mahi-mahi with pineapple salsa before serving.

Fish Chowder

Ingredients:

- 1 pound white fish, cubed
- 4 slices bacon, chopped
- 1 onion, diced
- 2 cups potatoes, diced
- 4 cups fish stock
- 1 cup heavy cream
- Salt and pepper, to taste
- Fresh chives, for garnish

Instructions:

1. **Cook Bacon:**
    - In a large pot, cook bacon until crispy. Remove and set aside.
2. **Sauté Vegetables:**
    - In the same pot, sauté onion and potatoes until softened.
3. **Add Stock:**
    - Add fish stock and bring to a boil. Reduce heat and simmer until potatoes are tender.
4. **Add Fish:**
    - Stir in fish, cream, salt, and pepper, cooking until fish is cooked through.
5. **Serve:**
    - Garnish with bacon and fresh chives.

Thai Coconut Shrimp Soup

Ingredients:

- 1 pound shrimp, peeled and deveined
- 1 can (14 oz) coconut milk
- 3 cups chicken stock
- 2 stalks lemongrass, bruised
- 2-3 slices ginger
- 1-2 Thai bird chilies, crushed
- 1 lime, juiced
- Fresh cilantro, for garnish

Instructions:

1. **Simmer Broth:**
   - In a pot, combine coconut milk, chicken stock, lemongrass, ginger, and chilies. Simmer for 10 minutes.
2. **Add Shrimp:**
   - Add shrimp and cook until pink and cooked through.
3. **Finish Soup:**
   - Stir in lime juice and remove lemongrass and ginger slices.
4. **Serve:**
   - Garnish with fresh cilantro before serving.

Salmon Quiche

Ingredients:

- 1 pie crust
- 4 ounces smoked salmon, chopped
- 4 eggs
- 1 cup heavy cream
- 1/2 cup cheese (such as Gruyère or cheddar), shredded
- Salt and pepper, to taste
- Fresh dill, for garnish

Instructions:

1. **Preheat Oven:**
   - Preheat oven to 375°F (190°C).
2. **Prepare Filling:**
   - In a bowl, whisk eggs and cream. Stir in cheese, salmon, salt, and pepper.
3. **Fill Crust:**
   - Pour mixture into pie crust and bake for 30-35 minutes until set.
4. **Serve:**
   - Garnish with fresh dill before serving.

Prawn Korma

Ingredients:

- 1 pound prawns, peeled and deveined
- 1 onion, diced
- 2 cloves garlic, minced
- 1 tablespoon ginger, minced
- 1 cup coconut milk
- 2 tablespoons korma curry paste
- 2 tablespoons vegetable oil
- Salt and pepper, to taste
- Fresh cilantro, for garnish

Instructions:

1. **Sauté Onions:**
   - In a pan, heat oil and sauté onion until soft. Add garlic and ginger.
2. **Add Spices:**
   - Stir in korma curry paste and cook for 1 minute.
3. **Add Coconut Milk:**
   - Add coconut milk and simmer for 5 minutes.
4. **Cook Prawns:**
   - Add prawns, cooking until pink and cooked through.
5. **Serve:**
   - Garnish with fresh cilantro before serving.

Lemon Herb Grilled Sardines

Ingredients:

- 8 sardines, cleaned
- 1/4 cup olive oil
- Juice of 1 lemon
- 2 cloves garlic, minced
- Fresh parsley, chopped
- Salt and pepper, to taste

Instructions:

1. **Marinate Sardines:**
   - In a bowl, combine olive oil, lemon juice, garlic, salt, and pepper. Marinate sardines for 30 minutes.
2. **Preheat Grill:**
   - Preheat grill to medium-high heat.
3. **Grill Sardines:**
   - Grill sardines for 3-4 minutes on each side until cooked through.
4. **Serve:**
   - Garnish with fresh parsley before serving.

Shrimp Ceviche Tostadas

Ingredients:

- 1 pound shrimp, peeled and deveined
- 1/2 cup lime juice
- 1/2 cup diced tomatoes
- 1/4 cup diced red onion
- 1/4 cup chopped cilantro
- 1 jalapeño, minced
- Salt and pepper, to taste
- Tostada shells

Instructions:

1. **Ceviche Mixture:**
    - In a bowl, combine shrimp and lime juice. Let marinate for 30 minutes until shrimp is opaque.
2. **Add Vegetables:**
    - Stir in tomatoes, red onion, cilantro, jalapeño, salt, and pepper.
3. **Assemble Tostadas:**
    - Spoon ceviche mixture onto tostada shells and serve immediately.

Grilled Tuna Steaks with Soy Marinade

Ingredients:

- 2 tuna steaks
- 1/4 cup soy sauce
- 2 tablespoons olive oil
- 1 tablespoon honey
- 2 cloves garlic, minced
- Fresh ginger, grated
- Salt and pepper, to taste

Instructions:

1. **Prepare Marinade:**
    - In a bowl, mix soy sauce, olive oil, honey, garlic, ginger, salt, and pepper.
2. **Marinate Tuna:**
    - Place tuna steaks in a dish and pour marinade over. Marinate for at least 30 minutes.
3. **Grill Tuna:**
    - Preheat grill to medium-high heat. Grill tuna steaks for about 3-4 minutes on each side.
4. **Serve:**
    - Slice and serve with extra marinade drizzled on top.

Fish En Papillote (Fish in Parchment)

Ingredients:

- 2 fish fillets (such as cod or sole)
- 1 zucchini, thinly sliced
- 1 bell pepper, thinly sliced
- 1 lemon, sliced
- Olive oil
- Salt and pepper, to taste
- Fresh herbs (such as thyme or dill)

Instructions:

1. **Preheat Oven:**
   - Preheat oven to 400°F (200°C).
2. **Prepare Parchment:**
   - Cut two pieces of parchment paper. Place fish fillets in the center of each.
3. **Add Vegetables:**
   - Top with zucchini, bell pepper, lemon slices, olive oil, salt, pepper, and herbs.
4. **Seal and Bake:**
   - Fold parchment over to seal. Bake for 15-20 minutes until fish is cooked through.
5. **Serve:**
   - Open packets carefully and serve immediately.

Baked Salmon with Honey Mustard Glaze

Ingredients:

- 2 salmon fillets
- 2 tablespoons honey
- 2 tablespoons Dijon mustard
- 1 tablespoon olive oil
- Salt and pepper, to taste

Instructions:

1. **Preheat Oven:**
   - Preheat oven to 375°F (190°C).
2. **Prepare Glaze:**
   - In a small bowl, whisk together honey, mustard, olive oil, salt, and pepper.
3. **Bake Salmon:**
   - Place salmon fillets on a baking sheet and brush with glaze. Bake for 15-20 minutes until cooked through.
4. **Serve:**
   - Drizzle any remaining glaze over the salmon before serving.

Szechuan Spicy Shrimp

Ingredients:

- 1 pound shrimp, peeled and deveined
- 2 tablespoons vegetable oil
- 2 cloves garlic, minced
- 1 tablespoon ginger, minced
- 2 tablespoons Szechuan peppercorns
- 1 tablespoon chili paste
- 1 tablespoon soy sauce
- Green onions, for garnish

Instructions:

1. **Heat Oil:**
    - In a skillet, heat vegetable oil over medium-high heat.
2. **Sauté Aromatics:**
    - Add garlic, ginger, and Szechuan peppercorns, cooking until fragrant.
3. **Cook Shrimp:**
    - Add shrimp, chili paste, and soy sauce. Cook until shrimp is pink and cooked through.
4. **Serve:**
    - Garnish with green onions before serving.

Fish Burger with Avocado

Ingredients:

- 1 pound white fish fillets, cooked and flaked
- 1/2 cup breadcrumbs
- 1 egg, beaten
- 1 avocado, sliced
- Burger buns
- Lettuce, tomato, and tartar sauce for serving
- Salt and pepper, to taste

Instructions:

1. **Make Fish Patties:**
    - In a bowl, mix flaked fish, breadcrumbs, egg, salt, and pepper. Form into patties.
2. **Cook Patties:**
    - In a skillet, heat oil over medium heat. Cook patties for 4-5 minutes on each side until golden brown.
3. **Assemble Burgers:**
    - Place fish patties on buns and top with avocado slices, lettuce, tomato, and tartar sauce.
4. **Serve:**
    - Serve immediately with your favorite sides.

Crab and Corn Chowder

Ingredients:

- 1 cup fresh or canned crab meat
- 1 cup corn kernels (fresh, frozen, or canned)
- 1 medium onion, chopped
- 2 cloves garlic, minced
- 4 cups chicken or vegetable broth
- 2 cups heavy cream
- 2 medium potatoes, diced
- 1 tablespoon olive oil
- Salt and pepper, to taste
- Fresh parsley, for garnish

Instructions:

1. **Sauté Vegetables:**
   - In a large pot, heat olive oil over medium heat. Add onion and garlic, cooking until softened.
2. **Add Broth and Potatoes:**
   - Stir in broth and diced potatoes. Bring to a boil, then reduce heat and simmer until potatoes are tender.
3. **Add Corn and Crab:**
   - Add corn and crab meat. Stir in heavy cream and heat through. Season with salt and pepper.
4. **Serve:**
   - Garnish with fresh parsley before serving.

Teriyaki Salmon

Ingredients:

- 2 salmon fillets
- 1/4 cup soy sauce
- 2 tablespoons honey
- 1 tablespoon rice vinegar
- 1 tablespoon sesame oil
- 2 cloves garlic, minced
- Sesame seeds, for garnish
- Green onions, for garnish

Instructions:

1. **Make Marinade:**
   - In a bowl, whisk together soy sauce, honey, rice vinegar, sesame oil, and garlic.
2. **Marinate Salmon:**
   - Place salmon in a dish and pour marinade over. Let marinate for 30 minutes.
3. **Cook Salmon:**
   - Preheat grill or oven to medium-high heat. Cook salmon for about 5-7 minutes on each side, or until cooked through.
4. **Serve:**
   - Garnish with sesame seeds and green onions before serving.

Zesty Shrimp Tacos

Ingredients:

- 1 pound shrimp, peeled and deveined
- 1 tablespoon olive oil
- 1 teaspoon chili powder
- 1/2 teaspoon cumin
- Salt and pepper, to taste
- Corn or flour tortillas
- Cabbage slaw (for topping)
- Avocado slices (for topping)
- Lime wedges (for serving)

Instructions:

1. **Season Shrimp:**
    - In a bowl, toss shrimp with olive oil, chili powder, cumin, salt, and pepper.
2. **Cook Shrimp:**
    - In a skillet over medium-high heat, cook shrimp until pink and opaque, about 3-4 minutes.
3. **Assemble Tacos:**
    - Warm tortillas and fill with shrimp, cabbage slaw, and avocado slices.
4. **Serve:**
    - Serve with lime wedges.

Seared Bass with Citrus Sauce

Ingredients:

- 2 bass fillets
- Salt and pepper, to taste
- 2 tablespoons olive oil
- 1/2 cup orange juice
- 1 tablespoon lemon juice
- 1 tablespoon honey
- Fresh herbs (such as dill or parsley), for garnish

Instructions:

1. **Season Bass:**
    - Season bass fillets with salt and pepper.
2. **Sear Fillets:**
    - In a skillet, heat olive oil over medium-high heat. Sear fillets for 4-5 minutes on each side until golden and cooked through.
3. **Make Citrus Sauce:**
    - In a small saucepan, combine orange juice, lemon juice, and honey. Simmer until slightly thickened.
4. **Serve:**
    - Drizzle citrus sauce over bass and garnish with fresh herbs.

Grilled Shrimp Caesar Salad

Ingredients:

- 1 pound shrimp, peeled and deveined
- 1 tablespoon olive oil
- Salt and pepper, to taste
- Romaine lettuce, chopped
- Caesar dressing
- Croutons
- Grated Parmesan cheese

Instructions:

1. **Prepare Shrimp:**
   - Toss shrimp with olive oil, salt, and pepper.
2. **Grill Shrimp:**
   - Grill shrimp over medium heat for about 2-3 minutes on each side until cooked through.
3. **Assemble Salad:**
   - In a bowl, combine romaine lettuce, grilled shrimp, Caesar dressing, croutons, and Parmesan cheese.
4. **Serve:**
   - Toss and serve immediately.

Stuffed Squid with Rice and Herbs

Ingredients:

- 8 squid tubes, cleaned
- 1 cup cooked rice
- 1/2 cup diced bell pepper
- 1/4 cup chopped parsley
- 1/4 cup grated Parmesan cheese
- 2 cloves garlic, minced
- Olive oil
- Salt and pepper, to taste

Instructions:

1. **Prepare Filling:**
    - In a bowl, mix cooked rice, bell pepper, parsley, Parmesan cheese, garlic, salt, and pepper.
2. **Stuff Squid:**
    - Gently stuff each squid tube with the rice mixture.
3. **Cook Stuffed Squid:**
    - In a skillet, heat olive oil over medium heat. Sear stuffed squid for about 2-3 minutes on each side until cooked through.
4. **Serve:**
    - Slice stuffed squid and serve warm.

www.ingramcontent.com/pod-product-compliance
Lightning Source LLC
LaVergne TN
LVHW081337060526
838201LV00055B/2695